How to Take Control of Your Asthma

RELIEVE THE SQUEEZE

by Peggy Guthart Strauss

photographs by Lucy Dahl

Viking

To my husband, Ed, and my family. And to my uncle, Dr. Ted Carrol, who has never let severe asthma stand in his way. —P. G. S.

VIKING
Published by the Penguin Group
Penguin Putnam Books for Young Readers,
345 Hudson Street, New York, New York 10014, U.S.A.
Penguin Books Ltd, 27 Wrights Lane, London W8 5TZ, England
Penguin Books Australia Ltd, Ringwood, Victoria, Australia
Penguin Books Canada Ltd, 10 Alcorn Avenue
Toronto, Ontario, Canada M4V 3B2
Penguin Books (N.Z.) Ltd, 182-190 Wairau Road
Auckland 10, New Zealand

Penguin Books Ltd, Registered Offices:
Harmondsworth, Middlesex, England

First published in 2000 by Viking,
a division of Penguin Putnam Books for Young Readers.

10 9 8 7 6 5 4 3

Text copyright © Draw A Breath Program, 2000
Photographs copyright © Lucy Dahl, 2000
All rights reserved

ISBN 0-670-89330-7 (hardcover)
ISBN 0-670-89339-0 (paperback)
Library of Congress Catalog Card Number: 00-043258
Cataloging-in-Publication Information is available.

Printed in Hong Kong
Set in Quorum and Kosmik

Foreword

"Will we lose her?" That's what we asked the nurse at Hasbro Children's Hospital in Providence, Rhode Island. Panicked that our daughter's asthma attack had gone too far, we had rushed her to the emergency room. Could she breathe? Were we too late?

Sophia's coughing had started with a cold just two days earlier. A simple cough. How dangerous could a cough be? We had been giving Sophia her quick-relief asthma inhaler and expected she'd be fine in a few days. As we came to learn, improperly treated asthma escalates quickly, and without proper treatment our daughter could have died. We arrived at the hospital just in time.

We learned asthma care the hard way—through a tough hospital stay. After months of struggling with Sophia's asthma, we realized that if we were having problems getting our child's asthma under control, so were thousands of other parents. There was a need for new materials for asthma education. This was our mission. First, we set out to build the innovative Draw A Breath Asthma Initiative at Hasbro Children's Hospital, driven by the efforts of Dr. Tony and Cathy Mansell, Dr. Anthony Alario, and a corps of world-class asthma experts who donated their time. Then we met Dr. Michael Rich, a kooky Harvard trained pediatric and adolescent medical clinician, and we knew he was what we needed for our video. His office looked more like a video studio than a doctor's office. His Video Intervention/ Prevention Assessment Program empowers kids to partner with their doctors to design their own asthma management plans. All together, we created the *Relieve the Squeeze* video and book for kids with asthma and their families.

We hope that this information can help others avoid scary trips to the hospital. Asthma can—and should—be a treat-at-home problem. It's no big deal if you stay on top of it and know what brings your asthma on. Partner with your doctor. Know your lungs. Be a meter reader with your peak-flow meter. Have your inhalers nearby. Always be ready to relieve the squeeze. It's all in this book.

Relieve the Squeeze will take you through the basics of asthma and what you need to know to take control of your particular asthma. If you control your asthma, your asthma won't control you.

—Lisa and Chris Van Allsburg

ASTHMA RAP

Late afternoon, city playground,
Kids are tossing a basketball around.
Air hangs heavy on the steaming blacktop.
The game is tied—no one wants to stop.

Taj gets the ball, he's ready to score.
Coach cheers louder than the traffic's roar.
Something's wrong—Taj is in trouble.
He drops the ball, coughs, bent double.

Coach is so mad—
    "Taj, are you crazy?
Get on your feet and
    stop being lazy!"
Taj can't move—
    he's coughing and wheezing,
His face is red—this attack's not easing.

Jared shouts, "It's asthma, Coach, he can't catch his breath
Taj needs his medication—it could be life or death."

Ambulance comes in a flash of noise
and light.
The EMT looks at Taj, says he'll be
all right.
She gets him on a stretcher,
puts a mask on his face.
Taj is breathing better now—he's won
this deadly race.

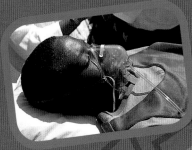

Coach and kids are smiling and relieved.
Coach says, "Taj looks so strong, I
wouldn't have believed
Such a tough player could be brought
to his knees
By mucus and coughing and lungs
that squeeze."

He shrugs his shoulders. "I guess Taj was for real.
I never knew asthma was such a big deal.
It's time for me to get an asthma education,
So that next time this happens, I'll have the
information."

Lots of kids have asthma, especially in the city.
Their numbers are growing, the statistics
aren't pretty.
In the playground the kids are playing ball some more.
And from now on their coach will always know the score.

Q. WHAT iS ASTHMA?

 A. Asthma is a disease where your airways swell up and secrete, or produce, mucus.

Most people don't think about the thousands of breaths they take every day. Breathing just happens, like swallowing or blinking. But for someone with asthma, breathing easily can be a big deal.

People who have asthma experience "episodes" where their lungs do not function properly. When something irritates their lungs, an asthmatic will often breathe noisily (WHEEZE), cough, and feel lots of pressure in their chest. For some people, these episodes happen all the time. Other people only have them once in a while. Either way, asthma is a serious illness that needs to be dealt with correctly as soon as possible.

Your lungs are vital organs, just like your heart or brain—you need them to survive. When you breathe in (INHALE), your lungs fill up with air, carrying oxygen into your blood. When you breathe out (EXHALE), your lungs release carbon dioxide, a gas made by your cells, as a waste product.

Each lung is full of small tubes called BRONCHI, which branch off into tinier tubes called BRONCHIOLES. Asthma happens when these tubes get irritated.

Things that bug your bronchi are called TRIGGERS. For some people, cat hair, the smell of fresh paint, or a cold might start the squeeze-and-wheeze. For somebody else, a moldy bathtub, a big test at school, or even something they ate for lunch can cause an attack.

> "The best way to describe an asthma attack is feeling like someone is sucking the air from your body."

When your bronchi, or airways, get irritated, they swell up and get narrower. Thick, gooey mucus can build up inside the tubes, making breathing feel like you're sucking peanut butter through a straw. Long, skinny muscles that surround the tubes tighten up during an attack, pressing on them. (Wrap a piece of sewing thread around your finger and pull—you'll see the squeeze.)

The squeeze, swelling, and mucus make it harder for you to breathe. More and more stale air gets trapped in your lungs until it's hard to breathe in or out. Carbon dioxide, which can be poisonous, builds up in your body, and less oxygen gets to the brain.

There is no cure for asthma yet, but you can learn to control your symptoms and lead a healthy, active life.

It's a fact: Asthma causes kids to miss school and go to the hospital more than any other illness.

Normal Airways

Air

Muscle

Bronchi

Bronchioles

Air Sacs

Enlarged cross section
of a bronchial tube in
normal breathing

Open Airway

Muscle

Airway Wall

Mucus

Membrane Lining

Airways during an Asthma Attack

Air

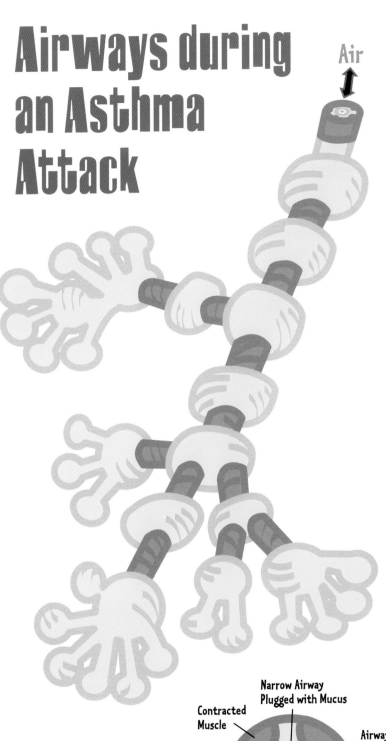

Enlarged cross section of a bronchial tube in an asthma episode

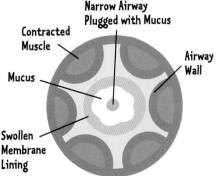

Narrow Airway Plugged with Mucus

Contracted Muscle

Mucus

Airway Wall

Swollen Membrane Lining

A. Anyone can get asthma at any time. People of all colors, shapes, sizes, and ages.

Most kids with asthma also have allergies. Even people without asthma can get the itch, cough, sneeze, and wheeze from allergies.

Lots of people don't let asthma stand in their way—teachers, movie stars, musicians, athletes, scientists—even firefighters. Your doctor can get you the information and medicine you need to stay healthy—but it's up to you to monitor your breathing and follow the plan carefully every single day.

There is some evidence that asthma is HEREDITARY—it can be passed on to you by a parent or grandparent. Just the way you can have the same color eyes or the same crooked toes as someone in your family, you can inherit asthma. You can't catch it like a flu, or give it to a friend.

It's a fact:

* More kids than adults have asthma—over five million kids in the United States alone. This is because some kids "grow out" of asthma as they get older.

* In big cities, one in six kids suffers from asthma.

* More African-Americans, boys, and kids who live in urban areas suffer from asthma than other people. No one is sure why.

SOME FAMOUS PEOPLE WITH ASTHMA

NBA star Dennis Rodman
Olympic track and field gold medalist Jackie Joyner-Kersee
Former president of the United States John F. Kennedy
Film director Martin Scorsese
Actor Jason Alexander
Entertainer Billy Joel
Baseball great Jim "Catfish" Hunter
Reverend Jesse Jackson
Olympic gold medal swimmer Amy Van Dyken
NBA star Dominique Wilkins
NFL running back Jerome Bettis

They've achieved amazing things, and SO CAN YOU!

 ONCE I KNOW I HAVE ASTHMA, WHAT CAN I DO ABOUT IT?

 Asthma episodes can happen any time, even in the middle of the night when you're asleep. That's why it's so important to learn the warning signs, monitor your breathing, and take your controller medication every day. Then your chances of an asthma episode go way, way down.

Q. WHAT ARE SOME EARLY SYMPTOMS?

A. Some kids will feel their symptoms before having an episode or "attack"—an itchy nose, watery eyes, a scratchy throat, or coughing. Others will feel their chest starting to tighten or congestion building up in their lungs. Sometimes, a person will feel cranky or nervous beforehand—everybody's different, so you'll need to pay close attention to your body to learn your early symptoms.

If the episode continues, more mucus will form in the lungs, you'll feel more squeezing in your chest, and you may start to cough or wheeze as you try to get fresh air into your lungs. If your airways get really tight, swollen, and blocked, you won't be able to cough *or* wheeze. Very little air will get in or out. Your lips may turn bluish, and it will be hard to walk or talk. Those are late symptoms. Get help right away.

"My doctor is probably one of the most important people in my life."

Two helpful medical terms you'll hear your doctor use are **CHRONIC** and **ACUTE**. Chronic symptoms and sicknesses are things you have all the time, or that come back over and over. Asthma is chronic—you always have it, even when you don't feel sick. Acute symptoms and sicknesses are more serious, and more dangerous. Asthma attacks are acute—they come on quickly, with serious symptoms, then end.

Asthma is no laughing matter, especially for kids—more and more people under 18 are being diagnosed every year.

There are many people with asthma who don't know they have it.

If you frequently wake up during the night coughing, tell your doctor. This might just be due to a cold—but it could also mean that you have asthma or your asthma is getting worse.

Know your symptoms.

Squeezing and wheezing
This asthma isn't easing.
I need a rest
From the pressure in my chest.

KNOW WHAT TO DO.

Having an asthma attack can be very scary. It's important to relax, think clearly, and take a puff from your quick-relief inhaler. Before an attack gets so bad that you feel you can't breathe, get medical help. Don't be embarrassed and don't wait to see if you feel better—*just do it!*

Experience will probably teach you when an attack is coming on, but it's a good idea to keep track of your symptoms in writing. For example, if a walk outside in the bitter cold or a fight with your best friend triggered your symptoms, write it down. Then, when you go to the doctor, tell him or her about your triggers. The next time you go out in the cold, you'll know to put a scarf over your nose and mouth. And the next time you argue with someone, you'll do some relaxing exercises to stop all your muscles from getting tense.

And there are lots of things you can do to stop your asthma attacks *before* they start. Get to the doctor and take your meds every day to stay healthy.

GET TO KNOW YOUR DOCTOR.

Most kids, and grown-ups for that matter, hate going to the doctor. The white walls, that medicine smell, and an icy-cold stethoscope are no fun for anyone.

But if you have asthma, your doctor can become your partner in fighting it. Together, you can come up with a game plan to treat your asthma in the best possible way. He or she can answer all your questions, teach you how to make your home more asthma safe, and show you how and when to take your medicines.

Q. DO I HAVE TO TAKE MEDICINE?

A. Yes. There are two different kinds of asthma medications: **LONG-TERM CONTROLLER** and **QUICK-RELIEF**. Controller meds work all the time to lessen the inflammation in your lungs and keep attacks from happening. Quick-relief meds work fast and are used when you feel an attack coming on or when you want to prevent one.

Controller meds are usually inhalers but can be pills, or syrup for kids who can't swallow pills.

Whether your controller medication is an inhaler, pill, or syrup, it will do the same thing. It keeps your lungs from getting irritated and swollen, so that your airways are open as wide as they can be. That way, when the airway muscles tighten, your tubes won't close or clog up as much as they might without the medicine.

Quick-relief meds are inhalers—also called pumps or puffers. They are filled with medicine that lessens the squeeze-and-wheeze by quickly relaxing the muscles around their airways. They work quickly and wear off quickly. Use your quick-relief puffer if you feel symptoms. Use it *before* you exercise or do anything that's likely to cause an attack. Carry one with you all the time. If your asthma is under control, you won't need it often.

"My asthma doctor is cool! He understands what I feel....He gives me a lot of attention."

You have to take your controller meds every day.

If you went to the dentist and didn't have any cavities, you'd still brush your teeth twice a day, right? It doesn't matter if you're feeling fine—make taking your medicine a habit. Do it every morning right before you brush your teeth. You need to rinse your mouth out after inhaling controller meds.

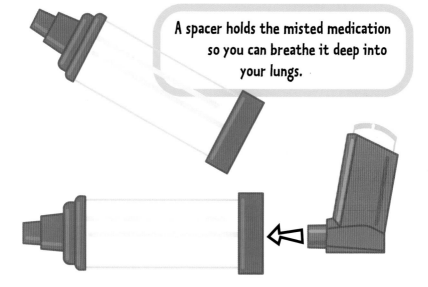

An inhaler looks like a small, narrow spray can that fits into a plastic case. There's a nozzle at one end, where the medication gets misted out.

A spacer holds the misted medication so you can breathe it deep into your lungs.

It's really important to call your doctor or get to a clinic if you think there's a problem with your meds.

Don't share your medications with anyone else, or use any meds that haven't been prescribed for you. Instead of helping, that could do major harm.

TRY A REMINDER:

Stick a calendar on your bathroom wall. Every day after you take your medication, mark the calendar so that you know you're ready to go.

You and your doctor can decide which medicines are right for you. You may need to try a few before you find the best one. Some might not take care of your symptoms enough. Others might make you feel nauseous or make your hands shake.

When you've found the combination of meds that allows you to feel your best, make a chart listing each one and when you should take it. Make sure that you know which meds are for emergency situations—highlight them on your chart in a bright color. Give one copy to your school nurse, carry one with you wherever you go, and put a third right next to your calendar on the bathroom wall.

USING AN INHALER IS EASY: Your doctor or a nurse will show you how to do it right. Practice in front of a mirror until you get the hang of it.

Q. CAN ASTHMA DAMAGE MY LUNGS?

A. Yes. It depends on what kind of asthma you have. Ignoring your symptoms or not treating them correctly can cause permanent scarring inside your lungs. Once your lungs are damaged, they will never work as well as healthy lungs. That's why it's so important to get medical help as soon as you have trouble breathing, to take your meds, and to stick to a treatment plan. If your asthma is going to get better, you're going to need to see your doctor as often as once a month until it's under control.

WALK ON BY.

It can be a big hassle getting to the doctor all the time, and you may be tempted to try out some of the non-prescription sprays that you can buy in drugstores. Don't do it: it's like trying to fix a flat tire with a piece of chewing gum.

AH-CHOOOOOO!
Squashing the Allergy Bug

Allergies are reactions our bodies have to things around us. Lots of things around your home and school can make you cough, sneeze, itch, or have an asthma attack.

Common Culprits:
Pollen, Dust, Mold, Certain foods, Perfume, Chemical fumes, Tobacco smoke, Furry pets, Cockroach spit (gross, but true!)

NEEDLES are nasty, but for some people allergy shots can turn allergies from a nightmare into a nuisance. Your doctor might decide to order allergy tests to see if you are sensitive to a variety of everyday things. If the mere sight of a cat, grass, or a dust bunny is enough to make you gasp and rasp, shots might help.

Once or twice a week, your doc will give you a shot containing a tiny bit of something you're allergic to. After a while, your body will get used to having that stuff around, and won't react to it so badly. With any luck, that will also mean fewer asthma attacks.

Allergy shots aren't for everyone. Usually, you need to have lots and lots of them before you start to feel better. And they work better for some people than for others. If your doctor thinks your allergies are a major problem for you, take the time to discuss with him or her any worries or concerns you have.

Some questions you might want to ask your doc about allergy shots:

Do they hurt?

How long do they take to work?

How many do I need to have?

How often will I have to get them?

Will they make me feel sick?

Can a shot cause an asthma attack?

Q. HOW CAN I ATTACK MY ASTHMA?

A. Your doctor can do a lot to help you, but in the end, it's up to you whether asthma will make you miserable or be a minor pain.

TACKLE YOUR TRIGGERS

Once you've figured out what things your lungs hate, you can suit up and go to war against them.

CLEAN YOUR ROOM!

Sorry to say it, but it's one of the best and easiest ways to beat asthma. All those things lying around are magnets for dust, mold, and other common triggers. They're tiny, but they can cause you giant-sized problems.

SURVEY YOUR SPACE

Your doctor or nurse will help you figure out all the ways you can get triggers out of your life, but here are a few good ways to start. With a pencil and paper, walk around your sleeping area. Is everything covered with dust? Do you let your dog or cat sleep on your bed or favorite chair? Is there a carpet on the floor? Are there drapes on the windows? Is there enough fresh air in your room? Write down anything you can think of that might be causing you problems.

Do these make you wheeze?

Cigarette smoke
Dirty clothes
Stuffed animals
Carpets and rugs
Furry pets
Feather pillows and quilts
Damp spots around windows and bathrooms
Piles of books, magazines, or CDs
Permanent markers, smelly glue or paint

Get rid of 'em!

Once you've cleared out the obvious offenders, keep it that way: dust using a damp cloth to keep particles from flying around; keep your window closed during your allergy season; wash your sheets in hot water every week; get special covers for your pillows and mattress. And if you have smokers in the house, tell them (politely) to take their dirty habit outside!

Often, finding and getting rid of triggers in your home can make a tremendous difference to your health. This doesn't mean you can stop going to the doctor, but keeping your space trigger-free is the single most important action you can take to improve—and sometimes remove—your asthma symptoms.

Remember: asthma is more than your lungs and nose—it's your life! Making simple changes to your lifestyle may be a drag at first, but the rewards will be worth it.

Q. HOW DO I USE A PEAK-FLOW METER?

A. A peak-flow meter is a small device you can get from your doctor, pharmacy, or clinic. To use it, you stand up, take a deep, deep breath, then blow into the mouthpiece as hard as you can.

The meter will show how clear your lungs are by measuring how fast air comes out. Keep a record of the number. Repeat this process three times in a row. After a few days, you'll see a pattern—your numbers will usually be about the same, with higher numbers on good days and lower ones on bad days.

Besides having numbers, the peak-flow meter is divided into three colored sections: green, yellow, and red, just like a traffic light. Your doctor will give you a plan for how to react to each color.

● Green is cool—you're good to go

● Yellow means caution—take things slow.

● Call your doctor if you see red—
Don't waste time—you could end up dead!

BECOME A CAREFUL READER

When your numbers are in the green zone, air is flowing through your lungs smoothly. You can go to school, play ball, sing in the chorus, and do all the things you normally do. Don't forget: just because you're feeling fine doesn't mean you can skip your meds.

If your numbers are in the yellow zone, you should be careful. Maybe the weather has changed or you have a cold. Whatever the reason, your lungs are a little more swollen and clogged than usual. **You might need to stay home from school, rest, and be extra careful to avoid triggers.** Follow the plan your doctor gave you or call your doctor. You need to get back to the green zone soon!

Red is the color you *never* want to see. Air is getting trapped *in* your lungs instead of flowing *out*, and you could be heading for a severe asthma attack— the kind that could land you in the hospital, or worse.

GET MEDICAL HELP RIGHT AWAY!

Learning to read your peak-flow meter is easy. Using one takes only a few minutes every day. It's small and it's simple. Leave it next to your toothbrush and use it just before you take your controller meds. Just as a thermometer can tell you if you have a fever, a peak-flow meter can show how clear your lungs are.

Make green your goal every day!

School, Friends, and Other Important Issues

Most likely, you're not the only person with asthma at your school, and you're certainly not the only person in your neighborhood. If you're feeling frustrated, freaky, or foolish for having asthma, it's time for a reality check. Remember Dennis Rodman, Billy Joel, and Jackie Joyner-Kersee? You are not alone!

An Inhaler is Useless if It's Empty.

Plan ahead to always have enough meds around. If you shake the inhaler and can't feel anything, it's probably empty. If you haven't refilled your prescription in a long time, it needs to be replaced. Get a new one from your doctor.

Q. HOW CAN i DEAL WiTH THE FEELINGS?

A. Feeling sad or stressed can really harm your health. Write stories, draw pictures, and let it all out. It sounds silly, but putting all the bad stuff on paper can really make you feel better.

Read up on asthma. There are lots of websites that provide free information on all aspects of asthma. Check out your local library for interesting books and articles. Learn everything you can— knowledge is your most powerful weapon against asthma—and maybe all that knowledge will pay off the next time you have a science report due! The more you know, the more control you can have over your illness. And the next time someone tells you that asthma is all in your head, you'll have the facts and figures to prove them wrong.

There's safety in numbers. If you know other people with asthma, talk to them. Compare your experiences and feelings. They might be able to share info about doctors or ways to cope. Friends who really understand what you're going through can give you lots of support, and you can do the same for them.

"This is a disease I control, that doesn't control me."

COOL FOR SCHOOL

Think of asthma as something that makes you stronger. Asthma teaches you to understand and listen to your body in a way that most young people never do. Taking medicine and following the plan you made with your doctor takes discipline. Be proud that you're tough, smart, and mature enough to do what it takes to keep your lungs healthy and strong. If you're comfortable with your asthma, it's likely that your classmates will be, too.

Don't keep your asthma a secret. Don't forget it's not your fault that you have asthma, and it's nothing to be ashamed of. Your friends, your teachers and school nurse need to know what's going on. Leave an extra quick-relief inhaler and a list of your meds in the school nurse's office. That way, in case of an emergency, he or she will know what to do.

It's harder to avoid triggers at school than at home. Keep several quick-relief inhalers around:

* **One in your locker**

* **One in your gym locker**

  or in the coach's office

* **One in the nurse's office**

* **One in your pocket or**

  backpack

Now you know
How to make the air flow—
Learn what triggers your attacks,
Do your homework, get the facts.
Take your medicine every day
Even if you feel OK.
Slow down when you're feeling stressed,
Know it's time to get some rest.
Charts and reminders help you follow
    the rules,
They can be simple, lifesaving tools.
Don't ignore your symptoms or push
    too hard,
You don't want to end up in the
    graveyard,
Know most of all that you're smart,
    strong, and young,
Now is the time to take control of
    your lungs!

Glossary of asthma terms

ACUTE–This word is used to describe illnesses or symptoms that come on quickly, and cause serious symptoms.

ALLERGY–A high sensitivity in your body to certain substances that can cause sneezing, itching, stinging watery eyes, coughs, rashes, and other irritations. Doctors who treat allergies are called ALLERGISTS.

ANTI-INFLAMMATORIES–Medicines that help lessen irritation in the air tubes. They can be inhaled, or taken as a pill or a syrup. Anti-inflammatories help swelling go down and cause the lining of the tubes to make less mucus. Most long-term controller meds are anti-inflammatories.

BRONCHI–The airways of your lungs. The smaller, finer tubes that branch off of the bronchi are called BRONCHIOLES. These are the twigs of the bronchial tree, the airways most affected by asthma.

CHRONIC–This word is used to describe illnesses or symptoms that you either have all the time, or that keep coming back again and again. You don't need to feel sick all of the time to have a chronic illness!

EXHALE–To breathe out.

HEREDITARY–Passed down from generation to generation in a family.

INHALE–To breathe in.

INHALER–A small device, also known as a PUFFER or PUMP, that allows you to get a measured dose of medicine into your lungs by spraying out a mist and inhaling it. It works much better if you use a spacer with it. Inhalers let you breathe the medicine right into your lungs—the source of the problems—so they work more quickly than a pill.

LONG-TERM CONTROLLER MEDICATIONS–These medicines keep your lungs from getting irritated or swollen on a long-term basis. You need to take them every day, even when you don't feel sick.

MUCUS–A thick, slippery substance made by the body's mucous membranes to protect and lubricate them. You may also know it as PHLEGM.

PEAK-FLOW METER–A small device that allows you to determine how clear your lungs are by measuring how fast you can blow air out.

QUICK-RELIEF MEDICATIONS–Medicines that work quickly, and wear off faster than long-term meds. They help to lessen or prevent acute symptoms, like an asthma attack, by relaxing and opening the airways. Also called SHORT-TERM or RESCUE MEDICATIONS or BRONCHODILATORS.

SIDE EFFECTS–Problems caused by your medicine. They can be minor or make you feel pretty sick. It's important to tell your doctor about any side effects you feel from your meds.

SPACER–A plastic device that attaches to the inhaler and makes it easier for the full dose of medicine to get into your lungs.

TRIGGERS–Things that irritate the airways in the lungs, often causing asthma attacks. Triggers may include tobacco smoke, food, chemicals, dust, weather changes, insects, cold air, pollution, mold—they're different for everyone.

WHEEZE–Noisy, whistle-like breathing caused by congestion, swelling, or muscle spasms in your lungs.

You can find lots of asthma information on the web. Lots of big websites that deal with health issues can tell you the basics. **Remember: information you get off the web is no substitute for going to the doctor.** Here are a few sites that have good information for kids and parents to look at together:

www.aaaai.org–The American Academy of Asthma, Allergy and Immunology. Their site offers lots of information and up-to-date news on all aspects of asthma and allergies, plus daily pollen and spore reports, and scholarships and contests for young people. Also provides free educational materials and a 24-hour hot line that gives medical referrals. Phone: 800-822-ASMA.

www.aafa.org–Asthma and Allergy Foundation of America. Provides listings of more than 150 local support groups for people with asthma and allergies nationwide. It also produces educational materials and newsletters. Phone: 800-7-ASTHMA.

www.aanma.org–National Allergy and Asthma Network/Mothers of Asthmatics. This organization offers a free information hot line, the latest news on asthma and allergies, helpful literature, and a monthly newsletter for members. Joining is free, but a donation is suggested. Phone: 800-878-4403.

www.allergycontrol.com–Offers a full line of supplies to assist in reducing allergen exposure in your home. Phone: 800-422-DUST.

www.cvs.com–CVS/Pharmacy and the Draw A Breath Educational Program at Hasbro Children's Hospital are partners in educating people about their asthma.

www.drawabreath.com–Part of Hasbro Children's Hospital's Department of Pediatrics, this innovative children's asthma program provides multidisciplinary educational materials for hospitals and schools, offers a summer overnight asthma camp for children, and mentors a children's asthma swim program. For more information, contact Draw A Breath Asthma Initiative via e-mail at this Website or call 401-444-8340.

www.fankids.org–Food allergy network. Teaches kids the ABCs of food allergies, with news, helpful hints, activities, and even ideas for school projects.

www.gazoontite.com–This site includes a library of articles about asthma and an on-line nurse who can answer your questions about asthma and allergies. It provides pollen counts for places all over the country. Also sells cleaning products, books, and even allergy-free toys.

hcpretail.honeywell.com–Website of the Honeywell Corporation, which makes air purifiers. Honeywell and the American Lung Association are partners in the national program to educate the public about the hazards of poor air quality.

www.lungusa.org–Web site of the American Lung Association. Includes a large section on asthma in kids and teens, including information on types of medication and instructions for using a peak-flow meter (with a peak-flow chart you can print out). The site also provides some of its information in Spanish. Many states have their own branches of the association, and you can find their addresses and phone numbers here. Phone: 1-800-LUNG-USA.

www.med.virginia.edu/medicine/clinical/pediatrics/CMC/tutorials/asthma/–Created by the University of Virginia Children's Medical Center. It has a long URL, but this is an excellent, simple site that presents information on kids' asthma with animated pictures, lots of helpful diagrams, and even lung sounds you can listen to.

www.medportinc.com–Medport manufactures and markets health-care travel organizers to transport medications including prescription and over-the-counter inhalers for asthma.

Acknowledgments

Our endless gratitude goes to Publisher Regina Hayes and Art Director Denise Cronin at Viking, who embraced this idea immediately; to our enthusiastic photographer, Lucy Dahl; to our deft author, Peggy Guthart (good heart) Strauss who researched asthma, top to bottom; to Ed Miller, who designed this gorgeous book; to Associate Editor Judy Carey, who kept us to our deadlines; to Tim Moses, the global horn who helped advance this book to families with asthma everywhere; and to Catherine Mansell, Director of the Draw A Breath Program at Hasbro Children's Hospital, and Dr. Michael Rich, M.D., of Boston Children's Hospital for their invaluable help in editing the text. A million hugs and kisses to the A-Man, Danny DeVito; to his co-star, Nia Long; to kid stars Milton Davis, Karina Barrero, Nicole Keyes, Dwight Mayfield, Mitchah Williams, and Stacey Meadows; and to all the kids with and without asthma who appear in the video and are quoted in this book, who believed in *Relieve the Squeeze*.

Without the vision of CVS/pharmacy's Chris Bodine, Stacey Deems, Jack Kramer, and Kate Shattuck, and the generous financial support of CVS/pharmacy none of this would be possible.

And to the following heroes of *Relieve the Squeeze*—the writers, directors and producers, doctors, nurses, parents, and children who brought the film and this book to you—bravo. Thanks to the huge hearts and souls of Dr. Tony Alario, Kenneth Arnold, the Child and Family Psychiatry Department at Rhode Island Hospital, Jerry Brenner, Cynthia Burns, Guyman Cassady, Wayne Charness, Ericson Core, Nancy Doyne, Doris Feinberg, Scott Flor, Joe and Melissa Gilbert, Merle and Stanley Goldstein, Hasbro Toy Company, Honeywell Corporation, Sharon Ingendahl, Jill Jaffee, Jake Karger, Armand Leco, Stephen Leeds, Robbie and Judy Mann, Dr. Anthony Mansell, Jay Miracle, Abe and Hilda Morrison, Dr. William Oh, Propaganda Films, Jennifer Rein, Fran Slutsky, Bill Teitler, Sophia and Anna Van Allsburg, George Vecchione, Myles Weisenberg, and Dr. Joel Weltman.

—Lisa and Chris Van Allsburg